At Home
In
Kansas

Enjoy!

Raymond S. Nelson

Raymond S. Nelson
7301 Galoway
Wichita, KS 67212

At Home In Kansas

Raymond S. Nelson

Art Work by Stan Nelson

Hearth

Hearth Publishing Company
Hillsboro, Kansas

At Home in Kansas
Copyright © 1998 by Raymond S. Nelson

First Edition
Printed in the United States of America

Cover photograph by Stan Thiessen

Library of Congress Catalog Number 98-75559
ISBN 1-882420-32-2

TABLE OF CONTENTS

AT HOME IN KANSAS

I am a Kansas transplant. Born in Brooklyn, New York, I came to the Midwest to attend college. But while I was a student, I met and married my wife Margaret, and we have since then lived in five of these midwestern states: Minnesota, Michigan, Nebraska, Iowa, and Kansas. We enjoyed each of them, but we decided to retire in Kansas.

I taught English for a total of thirty-nine years in two colleges, Morningside College in Sioux City, Iowa, and Friends University in Wichita. Retirement was a natural outgrowth of my twenty year stint at Friends. Margaret and I had become attuned to Kansas and decided to stay.

We think that Kansas has a big sky that rivals Montana's. We enjoy the wide open plains as we travel west, and we love the Flint Hills to the east. We marvel at the spectacular crevasses and hills in the Medicine Lodge area and natural towers in the Gove County region. The stereotype of endless dreary miles is simply not true. The scene shifts as marvelously as a chameleon. It depends on what you look for. Wheat fields or, at other times, tumbleweeds, are as fully glorious in their way as the trees and hills of New York State.

And a relatively small population has led in significant ways over the century. Women had the vote in Kansas before the country, Carry Nation and the WCTU helped precipitate the Prohibition Amendment (for good or ill), the Emporia Sage caught the attention of national leaders, Alf Landon and Dwight Eisenhower were national figures, and many more. Kansas has much to be proud of.

We enjoy the winters — milder than we had farther north. And the long growing season is a pleasure for those of us who garden. The only thing I wish different in Kansas would be a bit more rainfall; the semi-arid nature of most of the state requires a great deal of coping. But aside from that one reservation, Kansas is a great place to live.

Raymond S. Nelson

ROOTS

William Wordsworth, English romantic poet of the early nineteenth century, wrote of poetry as taking its "origin from emotion recollected in tranquillity." I agree to a point, but I would add that thought is just as instrumental in the generation of poetry. For emotion and thought blend, in my view, and these poems gathered in a section called "Roots" are the result of my having looked back over a lifetime. The poems in other sections are similarly informed by memory of course, but these seem to stand apart from those which are more focused on "family" or "faith."

Our current age is curiously fascinated with roots, as Alex Haley so well demonstrated. The rage for genealogy and antiques, both of which have erupted during the seventies, eighties, and nineties, gives evidence of a broad level of interest in history, pioneers, the frontier, and heritage. Even our environmental concerns underline our common wish to do a better job of caring for our cosmic home, recognizing that as a people we have been careless of sea, air, and earth. We have wasted our resources, and polluted our planet. These many cultural thrusts speak vividly of our shared interest in our roots.

HOME SCENE

These walls enclose my so familiar space,
A place of quiet comfort and retreat:
My son's oil painting in its proper place,
My mother's handwork on the rocker seat,
The mantel shelf awash with clock and vase
And glass and bowl and plate and woven wheat.

Loving fingers made most things I see:
Joe's plaque and Gordon's silkscreen on the wall,
Margaret's rosemaled "welcome," Johnny's free-
Styled scene, Grandma's afghan, Hilda's shawl.
Surrounded by such things so dear to me,
Alive to each, I pause to relish all.

I wander in these rooms by day and night
Aware of every table, lamp, and chair
Quite rooted to the spot that seems so right
For just that piece. We almost never care
To change a bit. Instead we take delight
In simple life-long things beyond compare.

REMEMBRANCE OF
THINGS PAST . . .

A silver spoon hangs
On my front room wall,
A gift in childhood from an aunt now long since gone,
And dainty porcelain coffee cups
Stand primly in a china closet row.

A crystal cut glass vase,
Now slightly cracked,
And wedding salt and peppers, plates, and bowls,
Fill up the shelves,
While candlesticks and lamps
Expand the treasures gathered through the years.

Just so much clutter
To the eyes of some
But not to me,
For with each gift of love exists a mist of memories,
A tie with those who've gone ahead
Yet live in these.

GANG AFT
A-GLEY

All summer long I'd watched the hazel nuts
Flesh out on head-high bushes. Dad and I
Took weekly jaunts, often taking cuts
Around the lake to where we said we'd try
To finish my log hut. Each lacy hull
Got plumper as the weeks wore on, light green
In color, changing slowly to a dull
Dry brown by early fall. I meant to clean
The branches, filling baskets with the fruit
I'd long thought mine. "They're almost ripe," I
said
To Dad. "Next week we kids will pick." To suit
Action to my words, I promptly led
My brothers to the woods. Not a nut
Was left! The squirrels got there first! They knew
Just when to pick the ripened store. We shut
Our baskets in disgust. Nothing else to do.

NOSTALGIA

They were a pair — the weather beaten barn
And ancient cider press — that greeted me
That splendid autumn day at Ollie's farm.
The barn was long and low, yet I could see
It had an upper and a lower floor.

I saw bushel baskets filled with fruit
Lined up along the ramp to the upstairs door,
But chose to wander on a lower route
Towards the open sliding door where sounds
Of tumbling apples merged with laughter. There
It was. The press, its oaken ribs fast bound
With iron rings, was being filled. The air
Was fragrant from the squeezings of the day
Before. Upstairs, I knew, were load on load
Of perfect apples, but around me lay
The windfalls, culls, and pippins on their road
To cider jugs that lined the nearby wall.

The pungent taste and heady fragrance still
Come back from just one bite, and I then recall
The hour I spent at Ollie's cider mill.

SALT HILL
CROTON-ON-HUDSON, NEW YORK

Salt Hill, they call it. A mound
Of earth a football field in length
And half as wide. Treeless, round
Or, rather, oval, with wiry grass
Not two feet tall to carpet all.
"A Viking grave," my father said,
And thought of Old Uppsala's sprawl
Of burial mounds, all lookalikes.

They stretch a mile in a gentle arc
From stately height to modest dune,
All measures of their fellow's mark
Of approbation, fame so served.
The Viking's ship became his tomb
All covered up with soil and grass,
For in Valhalla he'd resume
His far flung voyages and rule.

A Korean king was laid in state
Then covered high with a mound of earth
Whose size declared how small or great
His reign had been while yet alive.
His golden crown, his cup and dish,
His wife and servants, robe, and throne
Were all interred should he wish
Or need for anything beyond.

East and West agree, it seems,
On how to heed death's urgent call,
For life's realities and dreams
Lead to strangely similar ways
Though half a planet lie between.
Customs, races, seem deep down
To be alike in ways not seen
By most. They speak of ancient ties.

DREAM-SCAPE

"It's what I have in mind for us, my son,
A place we can enjoy together,
All of us. Together."
We were walking through a field,
The two of us,
And he was talking as he talked no other time.
We chose our steps with care,
Stepping over stones and tangled berry vines.
We crossed a stone fence partly down
From rabbit hunters, and trod a winding path
That took us down a hill and cross a marsh.
"Here will be one lake, the second by our cabin,
One on top the mountain, and one down there below,
Four lakes — a whole chain of them."
He was expansive, and I reveled in his pleasure
As he shared with me that Sunday morning,
For he talked as if I were an equal.
The land abruptly changed to trees and brush.
I followed close behind him on an ancient path,
Fending off the branches snapping on my face.
"When one gets low, you open up a valve
And fill the next one down," he said.
I shared his vision of the lakes and glory
Of the place (as it now was and it should be),
Absorbed in his glad voice, contented in his joy.
The brambles snagged my trousers,
While weeds and grasses filled my shoes with seed.
Yet we rambled on.
Father didn't seem to notice
My small troubles as I struggled to keep up,
Absorbed in his own thoughts and plans.

"I hope some day you can enjoy this place,
My son, when all this work gets done."
And I, with full heart said, "Sure, Pop,"
And meant it.
Many days have passed,
And many waters coursed the streams since then.
One lake was well nigh finished,
But things came up to stop the other three.
Then father died, and nothing more was done.

Years and miles have come between
That boyhood day and now.
Each child has gone a separate way,
And thought his separate thoughts.
Father's plans were left undone.
No man dreams another's dreams
Or brings another's dream to light.
His dream was his, entire,
Yet more precious in the sharing
Even with a child that autumn day
Than had he kept the vision in.

THE MIGHTY HUNTER

Isn't that a magnificent bird
There on the piano? I had it stuffed,
Oh, thirteen, fourteen years ago.
Ray was perhaps sixteen that fall,
Excited about Grandpa's twelve gauge.
Anyway, he'd been tramping around
The place by the swamp, by the lake,
Through the heavy woods, seeing rabbits,
Squirrels, partridge, pheasants, and got
The fever. He wanted to hunt.

He told me how he took the gun —
It was a double-barrel deal — and put
Some shells in the barrels and extras
In a pocket, then started off. He'd
Heard some pheasants crowing near
The flatlands, so he headed that way.
He walked and walked, he said, but saw
None. Nothing. But he kept on.

Finally it was late afternoon, but he
Decided to go across the highway
And try just a little longer.
There's a nice field there — lots of cover,
Some sumac and low bushes.
Well, he started to cross the field
And a rooster flew up, and away.

You know how noisy they are.
But Ray was ready, excited but ready.
He flicked the safety off, aimed
And shot. I forget if he said one shell
Or two. And the bird went down.

Heart pounding, he hurried on
And found the bird. Still alive.
So he cracked its neck, and started
Looking it over. No blood. No mess.
No broken bones. It was a beauty.
He took it home and his dad
Called a guy who mounts birds
And animals. Yeah, he could do it,
So they brought it to him,
And he did a nice job.

I've kept it there ever since.
Still looks good. Oh, a little
Dusty and worn, but pretty good.
Ray was really proud of it,
But it bothered him to look
That live, hurt bird in the eye.
He felt bad about it, and quit
Hunting after that. He hikes, he loves
The woods and birds and animals,
But doesn't hunt them any more.

ERRAND AT NIGHT

What dread of the dark I one time knew, I'll tell
On the chance you've been there too. My dad said, "Ray, I
need the bit we left in the woods by the well."
I had no choice, of course, but to obey.

The road was roundabout, and long, and steep,
Though bathed in early evening moonlit glow,
So I chose instead a path through a forest deep
To save some steps despite the gloom below.

The darkness hung about me like a pall
As I trudged with a coal-oil lantern in one hand
To find that bit we left at a half-built wall
In a grove of elms at the far edge of our land.

I felt the well-worn path beneath my tread
More than I saw beyond the feeble ring
Of light. Deep shadows loomed above my head
As I stepped slowly towards the walled-in spring.

I paused and leaned my weight against a tree
When, to my fright, the surface moved beneath
My hand. My hair stood straight, I turned to flee,
But frozen, saw a black snake underneath.

I was familiar with the vines that rose
On the rough elm bark. I'd rested at this place
Before in daylight on this path. Now I froze
In fright as the snake slid down at a steady pace.

I jerked away and ran in panic fear,
Though I ran to the well and wall. Not a moment to waste,
I found the tool, then found a way to veer
To the welcome moon-blanched road and got home in haste.

FAMILY

A plaque hangs in our home with the words, "Other things may change us, but we begin and end with family." Most would agree that family matters take highest priority in the scale of things. Now retired, Margaret and I take every opportunity to visit children and their families. We attend birthdays, graduations, weddings; we gather for Easter, Thanksgiving, Christmas, and every possible holiday between.

We have albums filled with photographs taken over the years, and we periodically look through them. We then laugh at early dress and expressions in some photos, but we also treasure the snapshots of those who have died and live on in memory. All of the prints are irreplaceable. We have portraits of patriarchs and matriarchs in our heritage room, and we are surrounded throughout the house with silver, china, crystal, art work, crafts, and furniture that are largely gifts from family.

I have a chest made of walnut lumber. The walnut tree was cut on a farm in southern Norway, sawed into lumber in Farsund, Norway, in the early 1840's, and made into three identical chests of drawers by my great-great grandfather. We use ours every day. The chest has passed from generation to generation, and when I no longer need it, one of my children will get it.

My mother's needlepoint graces a rocking chair in the front room, and a homemade storage chest that stands in our kitchen affords memories of Margaret's father. The kitchen table is scarred from countless children's school projects and wear spots from a move or two; it is well worn despite several coats of varnish over the decades. Margaret and I sleep in a bed that was a wedding gift from my parents, and chair after vase after lamp after table in our home have associations that enrich our lives.

All of these elements show how our lives touch and intertwine. Family life is at the center of our entire experience, and home base in Kansas is aptly the center of a world wide network.

MY MARGARET

The pearl of greatest price is she,
The gem of highest worth,
The diadem which crowns my life
And beautifies the earth.

EARLY FALL

Sitting with my grandson on my knee
Late one warm October afternoon,
I idly flicked a silver-gray hair free.
It fell like autumn's dying leaves, already
Falling round me from a maple tree,
One gray hair — emblem of mortality.

COURTSHIP

He preens his feathers, puffs his chest,
Croons a love song — she's impressed
(But she plays coy, she looks askance).
He tries harder, starts to dance,
He whirls and struts and tunes his voice
Until she's taken — he's her choice!

MARRIAGE

True marriage is a blending of two minds,
Two spirits become one. As oaks are made
More sturdy by the wind, each partner
Grows in strength through gentle pressure
And the shocks of life.

True marriage is a new embodiment,
Male and female sharing bed and board
And bringing forth the fruits of love
As God ordained from immemorial mists
For creatures here below.

True marriage is a giving and receiving,
Two lives that intertwine like vine and elm,
Supporting now, enfolding then, as each
Responds to each in weakness and in strength
While years in cycles roll.

HOME

The walls may be of marble
The walls may be of skin
The walls may form a fortress
Or seem just paper thin.

The rooms may run to twenty
Or be no more than one
What matters is the heart room
That makes a house a home.

MARK ANDREW

Oh Gift of God, dear Child of Grace,
On thy and our behalf, once more
We gather in this holy place
To offer thanks and God adore.

In spirit and in truth we share
The sacrament, the holy word;
We join in song and simple prayer
In promise that we shall be heard.

We meditate on earlier days
When Mark and Andrew walked the earth
And daily on Christ's face could gaze,
As we cannot — yet in your birth

(A mystery unplumbed, unknown)
The future spreads before our eyes,
The promise of an age to come,
New rainbow in these clouded skies.

Oh Son of God, though Child of Earth,
We consecrate ourselves, and you,
To seek these things of greatest worth
In confidence that God is true.

(Bulletin insert at the baptism of Mark Andrew
Nelson, March 1979, in First Covenant Church,
Sioux City, Iowa.)

FIRST STEP

We annihilated space today.
Distance crumbled into nothingness,
While spheres in orbit tumbled into disarray,
But fresh new worlds came into view
As Raymond stepped out all alone,
To meet, on sturdy legs, the new.

(Raymond Stanley Nelson III walked in
January, 1984)

TRUST

"Grandpa can fix it," the three year old said
As he handed his tractor to me.
"See? It's broken right here,"
And he added a shaft and two wheels.
He was talking to no one particular
— Perhaps to himself —
As he stood at my knee,
I looked at the pieces
And then at his face,
Then back to the wreck in my lap.
"Oh, T. J.," I started, then stopped,
As he tipped back his head.
I looked at his face,
His damp curls and blue eyes,
The confident set of his chin.
I wavered, and knew I must try.
"Why, sure, Little Fellow, let's give it a whirl,"
And I knew I must magic perform.

MY DAUGHTER

God loaned an infant child to me,
A talent to comprise.
She lived with me a score of years
And proved a precious prize.

She was not chattel, though my charge,
Not property, but free,
A trust the Lord of Life endowed
And left consigned to me.

She returned a hundredfold
Her worth in love and care —
Her steward, I am rich in soul
From tending one so rare.

MY SON

You are my immortality, my son,
And I bequeath my best. Look not to pence
Or sense to guide your steps each day from hence,
God will supply your need. With wisdom won
You'll learn to balance things of heav'n and earth
And thrive as steward of all things of worth
In life, to finish well as you've begun.

JACK AND CHRISTY

The rings you've given and received declare
The oneness of your lives from this day hence.
The gold is hallmark of the love you share,
The circle symbol of the permanence

Of nuptial vows. Unbroken bands bespeak
The flow of years between the words "I will"
And tottering steps of age. And as you seek
To live in harmony and peace, you'll fill

Each day with quiet words, with courtesy
(Like beams and boards that carpenters espouse),
To form the edifice that all will see
And honor as fulfillment of your vows.
Now link your rings to form a living chain
That will endure a lifetime's sun and rain.

THE EAGLE

Symbol of excellence,
The eagle soars with grace
Above the tumult of the world.

Symbol of solitude,
The eagle hunts alone
And rules from a mountain crag.

Symbol of might,
The eagle wrests his living
From a teeming earth.

Symbol of fidelity
The eagle shares an eyrie
With one mate and a pair of chicks.

(Matthew Nelson became an Eagle Scout in
                                    May of 1998.)

LOVE

"The more you give, the more you have,"
She said to John her son,
And spoke, her husband knew full well,
From wisdom slowly won.

He'd watched her meet the children's needs,
Mid fretful fevers, health,
Through midnight vigils, morning light
In poverty and wealth.

He'd known her constancy to him
Despite the storms of life,
The daily batterings, the wounds
She'd dressed as loving wife.

She'd given, given, given till
She had no more to give,
But having given all she had
She'd freed herself to live.

LOVE SONG

The softness of her hand in mine,
The curve of her smooth cheek,
A wanton wisp of hair . . . distract. . . .
Yet urgently attract.

A quiet strength shines in her eye,
Allure from her full breast —
The bloom of fairest womanhood,
The blush of all things good.

POP

He never threw a thing away,
"I'll find a use for it," he said,
"You'll see. It pays to save." Instead
He hoarded for another day.

He crammed the shed from roof to floor —
In fact things spilled into the yard
Where treasures he would not discard
Lay close at hand, a well-stocked store.

Old tin and steel and glass and wood,
Worn trucks and cars festooned with weeds
Were hostages to future needs.
They all in waiting order stood.

Few open spaces lay at hand.
We chose our steps through narrow ways
And dodged each item in the maze
While wishing hard for clearer land.

"I'll find a use for that," he said,
And often did. He fixed and patched
His tools and house, though rarely matched
Appearances (or cared a shred).

We had small patience with his way,
We saw the clutter and confess
We wondered how he stood the mess,
He smiled and let us have our say.

"It pays to save," was his exchange,
Then used his varied store to mend
Whatever thing he might attend.
He never felt the need to change.

PARTING

Destined to leave in minutes, I
Clung to my beloved, she to me.
The gate had cleared, the moment neared,
And soon we'd be apart for months.
"I'll write," she said. "And I," I said.
The words came slow, the seconds raced,
"It won't be long till I am home
Again," I said. "I know," she said,
"But home will be so empty while
You're gone." The words fell flat and dull,
As heavily as frost in May.
But as the final call drew near
I said, "My dear, the one moon shines
Both here and there. Let's pledge our faith
That when we see that silver orb
We'll think how we are one in truth
And love, despite the miles between."
A single tear rolled down her cheek
As she looked up, and said, "I will.
Though half a world may lie between,
Our common moon will make us one."

24

FAITH

Faith is a personal matter. And all people function every day on faith in each other and in our institutions. Faith is thus a very practical thing. We could not carry on without it.

We operate by faith in religious matters also. Our powers of reason are limited on every side, and our senses are sorely restricted. The wild animal can scent a human at a distance, for example, whereas we humans can not. And there is so much we do not know. Those persons among us who seem to know the most are quickest to admit their limits. We are thus surrounded by mystery on every hand.

That there is a creative God I do not doubt for a moment. Our world, our universe, and we ourselves are so marvelously conceived and realized that only an intelligent Creative Being could be responsible. The cosmos didn't just happen.

Dogmas may come and go, creeds may coalesce and vanish, rituals and rites may appear and disappear, services and practices and schedules may vary, but the message that a Supreme Being is in charge continues generation after generation. Though our doctrines and policies and procedures may vary from communion to communion, the church affirms the love of God and the need for each of us to love all others. Surely God, the greatest Mystery of all, is the foundation of the faith that allows us to serve God and each other with all our heart and soul and mind.

BEHIND THE VEIL

God is the circle squared
A sunbeam frozen fast;
God is voluble silence,
An atom punily vast.

God is bottomless height
A tower eternally low;
God is a jet black sun
Emitting a brilliant glow.

God is serene monsoons
Or blustery tranquil showers;
God is beyond our ken
Not less than my garden flowers.

MYSTERY

The Maker donned a robe of light
Neatly lined with shades of night
To shield himself from human sight
And work his will in sovereign might.

God's garment hides his essence true
From human grasp and human view
Because "to know" means "to subdue."
And Mystery — once known — is through.

LENT

Shrovetide paves the way for Lent
Inviting every penitent
Confess each sin and then repent,
Abandon faults and days misspent.

A pinch of soot, a palm leaf brent
Are symbols for the supplicant,
Of contrite heart, of mendicant,
Who come to God through sacrament.

Lent dramatizes man's intent
To live by simple faith, content
To know the Spirit provident
Of all things good and excellent.

GOOD FRIDAY

They stripped him and whipped him,
They laughed him to scorn
They bound him and crowned him
And mocked him that morn.

He viewed them and knew them,
He loved them like kin . . .
Addressed them and blessed them,
Forgave them their sin.

THE CROSS

Jesus staggered neath the weight
Of the rough-hewn, rugged cross
Till Simon was constrained to bear
The load. The clouds hung low, the day
Wore gray, as brutal soldiers led
The Lord of Life to pain and death.

His body writhed as nails drove home,
As weight tore flesh, and blood ran free,
A sorry sight that made the crowd
Draw breath and sigh in sympathy.
It was a cruel and bitter day
The Lamb of God endured alone.

I see the scene on Calvary
Through stark imagination's eye
And wonder how the jaunty gold-filled
Cross I wear on my lapel
Squares with the naked living Truth
Expressed that day on Golgotha.

THE EUCHARIST

The fellowship of Faith is one
Through common love of Christ, the Son,
And sharing at the sacred board
Helps everyone confess the Lord.

The silver chalice, ancient pyx,
The bread and wine and crucifix,
Arranged to serve the sacrament,
Are summons to each penitent.

The juice and rough-cut cubes of bread
The Bible, candles, cross instead
Speak just as plainly of God's grace
Though symbols in another place.

The cup of wine, the loaf of bread
Unite the church beneath its Head
In bonds Christ's broken body tied
When for mankind in love he died.

STARLIGHT

The stars shine clearly
Whether seen or not.
The sun may hide them,
Or the moon subdue,
But stars shine always
With a steady glow.

The Light dwells inly
Whether known or not.
It may be stifled
Or it may shine low,
But the Light is faithful
To the Maker's will.

DOXOLOGY

All nature is a hymn to God.
The liveliest rill, the lowest clod,
The placid pond, the hurricane
Join in a solemn choral strain
To match the music of the spheres,
A realm not tuned to human ears.

But hum of insect, song of birds
Blend into airs that can be heard,
That add to plaintive sounds of sheep
And cattle, moan of doves, the cheep
Of chicks, the howl of wolves, a round
Of notes which everywhere resounds.

All nature sings to those who hear,
To those, like Francis, who in sheer
Delight perceive the mighty voice
Of all creation raised in a choice
Motet, a harmony sublime,
Through all eternity and time.

MIRACLES

The day of miracles is here,
Not gone, as some would say;
It simply takes an eye and ear
Not dulled by custom's sway.

Each baby born, each seed that springs
To life in plant or tree,
Each wheeling planet as it swings
Means more than we can see.

Each pulsebeat, breath, or clasp of hand,
Each cut or bruise that heals
Is more than we can understand,
Hints more than it reveals.

We who live by faith must view
God's tapestry while spun —
A miracle is just as true
A million times as one.

HEALING TOUCH

A lonely woman, deep in debt
And desperate in her body's need,
Seeks help. She sees the Master' face
Yet dares no more than touch his hem —
That's all it takes!

A disobedient child outstretched
In tears, his hair and eyebrows singed,
His features burned, finds healing peace,
Forgiveness, in his father's arms,
And loving care.

A teenage rebel storms upstairs
In hopeless, speechless rage. But soon
A gentle knock, a "Don't come in . . . .
Come in." Then tears, a gentle touch,
And healing words.

A couple wander aimlessly
Within the maze of modern life
Till cancer strikes, and chaos reigns.
But they embrace, repledge their faith,
And overcome.

An aged man sits bolt upright
And stiff in his recliner chair
Remote from wife, from us, from all
Until I press his hand in love:
He presses back!

IRRESOLUTION

The alto's voice sang on,
And on — it held on Lord:
"The glory of the Lord is ris'n!"
The seventh chord hung on.

Resolve it now, I thought,
Reach the tonic. Come to rest.
Don't hold me in suspense,
Oh, Handel! Solve it now!

And, Lord, of whom she sang
Resolve this seventh chord
Of holocaust and death,
Bring in your day of peace.

Shall we indeed see lambs
Lie down with lions? Can bombs
Dismantled be, and lands
Lie lapped in worldwide joy?

Or is the vision vain?
Shall seventh chords sound on
The while the pride of men
Suspends a world in flames?

WORSHIP

I cannot remember a time when I was not involved in church. I remember being carried to church as a young child, and I have been active in Sunday School and Worship Services since those early years. I graduated from a Bible College and then served three parishes as pastor for a total of twelve years. And over the years I have participated in six different protestant denominations. All were good experiences.

I see God working in his creation around the world in many varied faiths, and I claim all people as my brothers and sisters. My four children worship in four different denominations: Catholic, Church of Christ, United Methodist, and Covenant. We all feel comfortable as we visit each other's homes and congregations and services of worship.

I see the church as the central dominant institution in America which forms and nurtures our common ethics and values. Families, schools and societies, corporations and individuals express our common morality, but the church is the source of such shared beliefs and doctrines.

The church is not always right, for the church is made up of fallible men and women, and always has been. Yet, on balance, the church has stood for goodness and right most of the time. When the church has erred, time and the common sense of perceptive people have restored the body to wholesome doctrine and practice. The two thousand year old institution sometimes flourishes and sometimes drifts, but western civilization is founded on her teachings. Quite properly, then, worship is an important part of American experience from week to week.

ON WORSHIP

It all depends. Some times are great,
And the altar moves with the
Power of the Presence. God's Spirit
Fills my mind, and my spirit
Is restored.

At other times the babies squall,
The coughers hack, the organ snarls,
The preacher drones, and little
Happens to uplift my thoughts
To serve my soul.

Almighty God is always there,
No doubt, to be discovered
In the silence or the sermon,
The anthem or the handshake . . .
It all depends.

OUT OF THE DEPTHS

Valleys rise to mountain tops
Yet bed the living streams that glide —
The springs and pools and brooks that flow
Between the heights on either side.

Sorrows soar, in time, to joy
As healing balms pervade the soul
Drawn from wells the Spirit fills
To help make wounded beings whole.

("There is nothing so sad in life as a wasted sorrow."
Elfrida Foulds)

GREAT GOD OF ALL

Great God of all, accept our praise
As we our mortal voices raise;
We own your majesty and power
In this, our brief but joyful hour.

We strive to be our best for Thee
Despite our earthbound minds, we see
The bounties of Thy grace each day
Yet never fully grasp Thy way.

We are not yet what we shall be,
Thy shaping is not done. So we
Endure Thy patient hand which still
Transforms us all with wondrous skill.

Framed in weakness, formed of clay,
We join our voices now to say
We worship Thee, our help and stay,
Eternal God: past, future, and today.

AT SERVICE

The open window let it all inside —
The fragrant honeysuckle, buzz of bees,
The gentle wind, the traffic sounds outside,
A mower's drone, a distant bark — all these
I noticed as I sat in church at ease.

I gave attention to the speaker's voice
Its cadence, rising, falling, like a song
I could tune out, tune in, as I made choice
Of where my thoughts should be allowed to throng
Or sense-distraction move my mind along.

I sang the hymns, I bowed my head in prayer,
I sat, I stood, I heard the choir sing.
I watched a child, his mother's braided hair,
A vagrant fly — before my mind could swing
Again to this day's worship of the King.

CROWN OF GLORY

Lives of thatch or lowly clapboard
Soar to mansions and a crown
If the spirits that inhabit
Them show love without a bound.

Lives of calico or denim
Yield to crowns in heav'n above
When simple homespun fabrics
Clothe such souls as lavish love.

MAKING A DIFFERENCE

I sometimes cringe in helplessness
To see the bulging bellies, sores,
The haunting eyes, the spindly arms
Of hordes of starving fellowmen.

I sometimes wonder, "What's the use?
With grift and graft and selfish hate
That stand between such people and
My little gift? What can I do?"

But then a quiet inner voice
Responds, "Don't try to do it all.
Do what you can. A single life
Restored outweighs the world in worth."

ORTHODOXY

When dogma takes the place of faith
And creeds become enshrined,
Then cant enshackles thought itself
And chains bind every mind.

HETERODOXY

When people dare to dream and think
And leave some things unsure,
Then they can walk by faith, and trust
The Spirit's overture

("Today's heterodoxy is tomorrow's orthodoxy."
                                     Father Josef Gregori)

DUSTY FOOTPRINTS

The Master wondered
As he wandered
In his sandals and a robe
Through the courtyard
Of a temple
Reaching high into the sky.

He viewed the pile —
The monstrous pile —
Of stained glass and of stone —
The buttresses —
The arches —
The icons and the spire.

He thought of life
In Nazareth
Of cottage and of shop
He thought of home
And daily chores
And simple daily meals.

He wondered
As he wandered
In his sandals and his robe
(Much as Socrates before him)
Whether men would
Ever understand.

"Why do they love
Such piles of stone,
Such vanity in glass?
How can they miss
The well marked ways
I outlined long ago?"

The Master wondered
As he wandered
In his sandals and a robe
Whether dusty feet
Might somehow soil
The great cathedral floor.

WHEELS WITHIN WHEELS

I contemplate the cycles
That govern daily life —
The ends and the beginnings,
The peace that follows strife.

I watch a storm to silence
While braving wind and rain,
Then revel in the sunshine
That floods the earth again.

Each dawn gives way to evening
And life succumbs to death;
My son becomes a father
While I draw shorter breath.

The seeds of spring grow golden
And harvest grains roll in;
The summer's sun arcs lower,
Ere winter's snows begin.

I pause in meditation
On Mystery and Power
Revealed in constant motion
And worship in that hour.

SEASONS

Kansas is blessed with four distinct seasons, and we make the most of each of them. Most people have preferences. Some enjoy snow and winter sports while others enjoy the warmth of summer. Most opt for spring and fall as favorites because temperatures are usually moderate and rainfall is plentiful.

I enjoy gardening, so I love spring as a time of preparation, planting, trimming, seeding, and all the other rituals of flower production. I appreciate the rains and even the storms that come our way. Summer too is a delight because then I can enjoy the blossoms, the fragrances, the colors, the respite from a more demanding fall and winter schedule. Actually, every season has its rewards.

Holidays become part of each season. The Fourth of July is hot and festive, while the ice and chill of winter seem appropriate to a fur-clad Santa and his reindeer. Surely we have simply accommodated weather to our expectations for each holiday. So it is with all our holidays: Christmas, New Years, Easter, Mother's Day, Thanksgiving, and all the rest. We know pretty much what to expect in weather for every special day.

SPRING

The crocuses and daffodils
Announce with trumpet sound
The resurrection of the land
As sunshine warms the ground.

The lilacs and forsythias
Their voices join in time
And redbuds, tulips, roses, flags,
Add their melodious chime.

Returning robins build their nests
And cheer us with their songs
The raucous jay, the meadow lark,
Enhance the choral throngs.

The gutters gush with swirling rains,
The thundrous drumbeats roll,
Lightning crackles, fields stand full,
And waters drench the whole.

And then the elements all fuse
In one symphonic blend,
The prelude to glad summer's reign
And song of winter's end.

MOTHER

A mother is a "female parent"
Says my English lexicon.

Of course.

But mine
Heard childhood sorrows,
Soothed nightmare frights,
Bathed feverish brows,
Cooked special food,
Baked birthday cakes,
Bought perfect presents,
Gave from a slender purse,
Mended shirts and socks,
Sang favorite songs,
Told endless stories.

What then is mother?
She's God's vicar in my life.

MOM

A strong link in the chain of life is she.
She's filled her place with gentle force for eighty years,
Her golden crown the hallmark of her quiet sway.

Coming half a sphere to this New World,
She's forged a character by which she's lived
In plenty and in want with daily dignity and grace.

Her man was irrepressible, creative, bold . . .
A sturdy pioneer of sorts . . . yet totally dependent on
Her love, attention, care, concern, and strength.

She carried water, cooked and laundered, canned and gardened,
Cleaned and mended, kept the house . . . surviving strain and stress;
She's tempered alloy of fine-carboned stainless steel.

Six links engage the future from the pattern of her past,
Assert fulfillment through a faithful life well spent
As "then" and "now" fuse clearly in her view.

Eighty years see change and storm and pain,
While eighty years bring wisdom, peace, and calm,
For eighty years view things not piecemeal, but in whole.

(Gudrun Nelson celebrated her eightieth birthday
on July 10, 1978.)

SUMMER

Flickering shadows, mountain lakes,
A fishing pole in hand
An icy jug, a pebbly bank
Suggest "Vacationland!"

A land of hummingbirds and bears
Of parks and pools and trees,
A land where cabins line the roads
And patrons take their ease.

The seashores lure their share of folk
To bathe and tan and dine,
To sail and ski and fish and surf
In mist or bright sunshine.

The central plains and lowlands cry
Their wares for summer dreams,
They offer woodlands, trails, and fields
And rivers, ponds, and streams.

The great migration ebbs and flows
Each year in surging droves;
From hill to plain and back again
Each restless wanderer moves.

AUTUMN

All nature slowly comes to rest,
Vitality grows numb,
The summer sun grows slowly cold
Till Autumn's fully come.

A trace of wood smoke in the air
And yards all cleaned and clear
With plants and flowerbeds tucked in—
These say the season's here.

A wedge of geese flies honking by
En route to warmer lands
While crowds of blackbirds twitter loud
In noisy one-night stands.

Some fields lie plowed and harrowed clean
While others wait for care
In stubble, fodder, hay, or grain,
Til springtime's milder air.

The earthtone hues in full array
(The reds and browns and gold)
Give hint of God's creative joy
In decking out earth's mold.

GOD OF THE HARVEST

With apples picked and safely stored,
With wheat and corn and milo in,
We gather in Thy house, Oh Lord,
To offer thanks for everything.

We share Thy bounty at our board,
We lift our eyes to Nature's pride —
The season's harvest, Autumn's hoard —
And worship Thee — Thou dost provide.

We revel in each russet sash,
In maples crowned with crimson crest,
In reds and golds from frosty lash
Which warn of winter's coming rest.

We watch, we pray, we seek Thy face,
In all Thy matchless handiwork
We sense Thy care, we claim Thy grace,
We seek Thy signature to trace.

WINTER

The snow, like frosting, decks each roof
And muffles all the sounds;
It garlands every post and shrub,
It swirls and drifts in mounds.

A tree limb silhouettes in gray
Against a leaden sky
As straggling leaves dip here and there,
Mere shreds of days gone by.

The whistling wind cuts through warm coats
And pierces gloves and skin,
It harries those who stay outside
And forces many in.

A sparrow on the shoveled drive
Gleans morsels to be found;
A squirrel loudly scolds the cat
Which stalks him from the ground.

The hibernating earth rolls on
In cozy slumber lain
Till vernal solstice thaws the ice
And springtime stirs again.

IN THE BEGINNING

In the beginning was the Thought,
The germ idea of what could be,
A world conceived to be so wrought
God's vision might fruition see.

In the beginning was the Word
The Utterance of God to man,
The Logos which this heart has stirred,
Declaring His primordial plan.

In the beginning was the Deed,
The fusion of God's Thought and Word
The ground of life, productive seed
Through which his mighty voice is heard.

THE FEAST OF LIGHTS

The winter solstice, darkest of the year,
Is the setting for the Prince of Light.
Flickering candles, burning bulbs, cheer
Us mortals through each long December night.

Life embraces both, the dark and light,
For pain and sorrow, joy and peace engage
In constant struggle for the victor's right
To claim the crown. It's so in every age.

A CHRISTMAS REVERIE

The five foot hemlock was our tree
That Christmas, rounded with a limb
We'd drilled in place.

Each bough hung low
With fancy bulbs and popcorn strings,
With nuts and candy canes and fruit
And tinsel fronds, but best of all
There were small candles placed with care
To burn in splendor on the boughs.
The yellow flames burned bright and danced
Both on the tallow and each sphere
That hung in place.

We children chose
An ornament that dazzled us
And made us think of wonderland.
My treasure was a silver bell
That tinkled softly at my touch
When I passed by.

The scene remains
And speaks, across the years, of light
That shone that night in Galilee,
Declaring peace, God's gift to earth.

CHRISTMAS EVE

The chores all done, we children washed
And dressed by five o'clock. At last
We gladly heard the call, "Come eat,"
And took our places at the festive board.
The food was simple — rice in milk
(With a hidden almond nut and prize)
Potatoes, meatballs, fruited breads
And cookies, cream and cherries, nuts
And dates. Then father read from Luke.
We heard, but thought he'd never end —
Our minds were on the Christmas songs
We'd sing while holding hands around
The tree, and after that, the gifts.
Someone played Santa Claus to pass
The gifts; then each one quickly tore
The tissue from the treasure troves
And, after noisy sharing, went
As slow as snails to bed and sleep.

THE NEW YEAR

The year peers from its Janus head
To survey stops and starts,
Recall the fate of hopes and dreams,
And ponder human hearts.

It asks about old wornout days,
Assesses shreds and shards,
It joys to find rich vessels there
Still whole among discards.

It focuses on distant goals,
It fashions precious things,
Affords a twelve-month void to fill
With treasure fit for kings.

WORK

"A perpetual holiday is a good working definition of hell," said George Bernard Shaw. Profoundly true. Nothing to do means boredom, tedium, meaninglessness.

Wholesome work is a necessity for well integrated human beings. Work can be physical labor or mental application, and a blend of the two is best. But people need to have some means of self-expression through work. It may be crafts, hobbies, position, job, chores, or any combination of these. But everyone needs a sense of fulfillment through application and commitment.

Some people believe that work is a curse, but nothing could be further from the truth. Production is a blessing available to everyone; work is essential to wellbeing. And when we think carefully about it, we spend more time consistently at work than at any other thing — except sleep. How wonderful it is, then, to enjoy productive hours and to realize how formative those hours are.

Happy are those people who find joy and meaning in their work, from cleaning to clerking to teaching to typing to keeping house.

A LA MODE

Just rack the language. Peel the skin
From words. Stretch and squeeze them in
To strange forms. It doesn't matter; it's
A poem. Force the pulp to new odd fits.

Twist the syntax, bruise the limb
Of sense. Let the poet beware — or sin.
Poetry must be, not mean, we're told.
And that means — well, who would be so bold?

SPELLBOUND

The blank white page upon my lap
Stares brazenly at me, a sneer
Upon its lips as I uncap
My pen, disposing me to peer
Around for things that must be done
Before inspired lines can fill
The white expanse that surely none
But I can momently distill.
I straighten bookshelves, dust a plant,
Then fill a cup with tea. I try
To organize my thoughts, but can't
Quite settle down to face those eyes.
At last, the chores all done, I make
Myself sit down, pick up my pen
To write a line — the spell to break —
And write another, and again.

OLD AGE

My battered book resists
The ravages of time.
The dog-eared pages serve
Despite the marks and grime.

Its spine is firm, though skinned
From constant wear and use,
Its signatures complete
Though flexible and loose.

The cover's lost its gilt,
The corners now are frayed —
Yet offered something new,
I'd never, never trade.

DROUTH

Tendance without love
Or service without care
Is like clouds without rain
Or croplands brown and bare.

SWEEP HAND

I said to her, I said, "I go to work
On Monday morning, and next I know
It's Friday afternoon." "Yes," she said,
"Time does speed by. I'm hardly done
Each day before I start again."

Time crept when I was young.
Hours seemed days, and minutes hours.
The hands on the clock stood still,
And Christmas never came. Neither did
The other special days I waited for.

Time is now a meteor, streaking hard
Across the sky, and I lone watcher
On the plain.   Time is the sped arrow,
The stooping sparrowhawk, the airplane
Hurtling through the night, the falling tree.

I reach my desk on Monday, and the rest
Is all a blur: a whirl of memos,
letters, lunches, meetings, classes, phone calls
programs, speeches, bedtimes, dinners, till I
look up — aghast — on Friday afternoon.

THE DAILY ROUND

A clock is, like a nagging wife,
A tyrant and a scold.
It won't allow in daily life
A moment uncontrolled.

Mealtime, worktime, playtime, bedtime,
The voice insistent drones,
"Do this!" "Do that!" "Come here!" "Go there!"
In strident, crabbed tones.

The orders issue from the face
Impassive on the wall,
And docile members of the race
Obey the imperious call.

WORK IS WORSHIP

I'm wonderfully tired, Lord.
I've pruned and hoed,
Watered, weeded, trimmed some trees
Since early dawn.

I'm like those early cloistered monks,
My Lord, who said
"Work is worship," then
Gave their all.

I thank you for the health and strength
That lets me tend
To daily chores. To praise your name
I offer . . . work.

LIFE

What an inclusive category! It holds everything! It reminds me of John Henry Newman's story of a schoolboy told to write an essay on the proposition "Fortune favors the brave." But Robert, says Newman, missed the proposition and wrote aimlessly, pointlessly about "fortune." "It would have been very cruel to have told a boy to write on 'fortune,'" Newman added; "it would have been like asking him his opinion on things in general."

Yet the label *life*, broader even than *fortune*, seems to fit the group of poems that follow. They may indeed comment in some way on Thoreau's memorable words:

> I went to the woods because I wished to live deliberately, to front only the essential facts of life, and see if I could not learn what it had to teach, and not, when I came to die, discover that I had not lived. I did not wish to live what was not life, living is so dear; nor did I wish to practice resignation, unless it was quite necessary. I wanted to live deep and suck out all the marrow of life.

Although Thoreau was of a different time and place, any Kansan, any person, can agree that "living is so dear," and make the most of every waking moment. Life is a great gift; the thoughtful person accordingly approaches each day in anticipation.

AT BIRTH

An infant is a glorious dawn,
A cropland newly tilled,
A vessel launched on unknown seas,
A promise unfulfilled.

Each dawn must run its course till dusk,
Each field its harvest yield,
Each vessel find its harbor home,
Each promise be revealed.

New life is daybreak of an age,
Is fertile field just sown,
Is voyage on uncharted seas,
Toward destinies unknown.

TRACINGS

As you write the story of your life
And pen one line and then another,
Have you left white space
At the margins of each page?
And have you left sufficient space
Between each line?
Don't blacken every hour with deeds.
Let your spirit soar aloft
Through spaces left unpenned
Among the lines of cursive script
That largely hold the tracings of your life.

MEMORIES

I write my sorrows in the sand
Or surface of a lake;
They slowly vanish from my sight
And hardly leave an ache.

I carve my joys in adamant
In letters bright and tall,
Encouraged then through memory's voice
To face what may befall.

AT SYMPHONY

Halfway through the movement's desert fare
One passage bloomed in sudden beauty, rare
And perfect in the blend the artist's care
Achieved in rhythm, timbre, range, and air.

That moment made the whole worthwhile, so fair
In essence that my spirit soared in prayer,
Borne up by strong emotion, unaware
Of all but stunning sounds beyond compare.

KNOW THYSELF

You cannot live another's life
Nor die another's death;
You cannot look through other's eyes
Nor breathe another's breath.

You yourself must look and breathe
And live and die alone,
Creating daily what you are
And what you will become.

CARPE DIEM

All our yesterdays are filed away
In photos, mem'ries, and the scores of things
That fill our treasure chests. So, live today.
Its all we have. Commoners and kings
Stand equal at the threshold of each day.

Tomorrow is a phantom. It may or may
Not be. This moment is reality
And calls each soul to dream, then freely play
The game of life — each day can then well be
A playing field where winners wear the bays.

Scan the stars at night, the sun by day.
Touch a tree, some grass, or blossom. Taste
A plum, an apple, or a date. The way
To win is through such simple things not based
On fortune, rank, or what the hucksters say.

And living calls for loving too. Do stay
In touch with family, then friends, a mate
Perhaps, and learn to love from early days.
The Wind of God blows through us to create
A caring fellowship. So, seize the day.

LIFE RUNS OUT

Life runs out like sifting grain:
It spots the earth like golden rain,
Pouring in a steady stream
From some lower grainbox seam.

Children heedless go their way
Happy in their careless play,
Sustained each day with love and care
They know will simply just be there.

Youths move further to the west,
Restless in their endless quest
For sense and meaning, seeking well,
Though dazzled by the moment's spell.

Men and women play their parts,
Act their roles, in fits and starts,
Pausing seldom mid-career
To ask of whither — there? or here?

Even age moves steady on
Night by night, and dawn by dawn,
Too frail to struggle much, or sing,
Condemned instead to limbo's ring.

Life runs out like running grain:
It seeds the earth in golden rain,
Dropping, falling to the plain
Unnoticed, till the box is drained.

COMPOSING STICK

Life is composed
   Piece by piece
      Day by day
         Of trifling little acts
            With here and there a main event.

Take
   A birth
      A desk
         A cap and gown
            A printing press
               A wedding cake
               A child or two
                  An anniversary plate
                  A death

And fit in all the sleeps,
The breakfasts, lunches, dinners, trips,
The clothes and chores and colds,
Until these fully cram the stick,
The composition done.

MEMORIAL

When day is done, and goals near won,
We pause in welcome rest and leisure,
With body bent, life almost spent,
We reckon up our earthly treasure.
What is our life, lived in such strife,
Amid incessant years of trouble?
Can we take heart, this scene depart,
And leave an edifice? Not rubble?

What shall we leave, when loved ones grieve,
As monument to our existence?
Shall granite stone, or deeds alone,
Attest to faith and hope's persistence?
When breath has ceased, the soul released,
Shall fit memorial be rendered?
Will thoughts of love, enshrined above,
A tribute to our lives be tendered?

AT HOME IN KANSAS

Margaret and I have enjoyed every state we've lived in, but we've chosen to retire in Kansas. When we bought our home in Wichita in 1976 we thought we would stay here temporarily. We expected to return to Iowa in retirement. But our ties in Iowa gradually weakened while the connections in Kansas became stronger. To stay in the heartland of the country, somewhat equidistant from our children and grandchildren, seemed right.

We enjoy the people, we like the local way of life, and we like the environment. Winters are not severe, and summers are usually pleasant. Spring and fall are our favorite seasons. All things considered, we are comfortable with our decision to stay in Wichita.

AT HOME

To share my days with Margaret, my wife,
In simple tasks around the house and yard
Within these twilight hours of my life
Is Eden, filled with fruits and joys unmarred.
There are burdens, true, as powers wane,
Concerns for loved ones ranged around the earth
And patient daily bouts with aches and pain,
But troubles plague all mortal days from birth
And, nothing new, we temper care with hope.
We trust in God whose kin we are, and face
Each day with thanks for strength and will to cope
With problems we can trim to commonplace.
Retirement with a beloved mate,
In short, blends all into a pleasant state.

DAYLILIES

Our yard is ringed with flowerbeds,
A spectacle of vivid hues.
The lilies lift their glorious heads
Each day in season, as they choose,
From fans of slender dark green leaves.
We seldom cut the scapes, for buds
In hundreds silently bequeath
The future's wealth of blooms — in floods!
We do, however, choose some blooms
And place them in tall fine-stemmed bowls
To add a grace to several rooms.
Their beauty stimulates,
Yes, captivates, the soul!

FORECAST

"Don't like it?
Stick around. It'll change."
Kansans chant this chorus,
Verse by verse,
To any visitor who comes this way
And wonders at the weather
(for the range of contrasts
Is a source of pride). Converse
Yet more, and still the tune resounds:
"It just won't stay."

Tis true.
The bitterest of winter's snow
Melts quickly in a day or two.
The heat of summer sometimes lasts,
But just as true,
A sudden shower brings a wind to blow
Oppressive heat away.
As moments fleet throughout the day,
Just wait:
A change is always due.

HIGHWAY 96

It winds across the state
From Columbus in the east
To Tribune in the west.
It twists and turns from Independence to Great Bend,
Then straightens with a flounce
To bring the traveler on his way
The quickest and the best
Despite the fact the route is mapped in blue.

It cuts the flint hills quite in two,
Its hills and valleys glorious to view,
Then plies its westward way along two rivers
For a change.
The open spaces that ensue
Embrace the grandeur of the plain
With earth and sky stretched wide
To enfold the wheat and cattle range.

The south wind rolls the tumble weeds
Across its path,
Till north winds send them back again.
The red-tailed hawks
Keep watch along the way
And deer emerge at dusk
With luck or loss their due.
The birds and animals and men
Respond to its allure
By night and day.

SEEDTIME

When winter's frosty ground
Becomes the loam of spring,
The daffodils and tulips raise their heads
In jaunty bloom
To welcome home our robins,
Harbingers of lambent days.

The trees leaf out,
The lilies long asleep bestir themselves
As foliage fills each bed;
The lawns green up
And vines begin to creep
As seasons change
And Nature gads about.

The wakened yard
Invites the dweller out
To dig and till and rake and trim and mow,
To tend the soil
With simple toil
Without a thought of livelihood,
Of kin, or woe.

WINTER GUESTS

They fly over every morning
Just about at seven,
Honking on their way to forage
In the fields:
Canadian geese.
They fly in wedges,
Each in perfect place.
Stately birds, they congregate
On barren river banks
To add a grace that
Only life can give.
They winter on the river
Till northern breeding grounds
Recall them to their vernal tryst.

PRAIRIE SCAPE

The horizon marks the seam
Produced by earth and sky
When sutured by my eye
On the far flung Kansas plain.

The air is crisp and clean,
So soil and field and grain
And tree, in sun or rain,
Create this pristine scene.

The crystal canopy
That arches day and night
Above this space invites
The viewer pause — and see:

There's beauty in these plains,
A glory all their own,
A place that we have grown
To love — it's in our veins.

THUNDERSTORM

Lightning crackles in the sky,
Scrabbled lines of brilliant hue,
Dancing arrows, silver-blue,
Striking earth or clouds on high.

Thunder follows sure as death
Sometimes early, sometimes late,
Rumbling, grumbling in a spate
Of claps and growls and bursts of breath.

There's little time for normal goals
Between the spectacle and sound,
For pounding pulse and frights abound
When lightning strikes and thunder rolls.

RAINBOW

A dewdrop on a blade of grass
Refracts the morning's eye
As fully as a waterfall
Or shower in the sky.

The bow draws wealth from leaden skies
And diamond rays from dew —
Pure joy lies close to sorrow's side,
And may from pain ensue.

CORNUCOPIA

This last section is less focused. It embraces a wider range of subjects, yet the poems seem worth sharing. Raoul Wallenberg needs to be remembered for his heroic efforts to aid the Jews of Hungary as World War II was winding down. He saved thousands of lives.

The playful trifle "Skin Deep" belongs somewhere and "Self-Sacrifice" is an exercise in one rhyme. "Angel Unaware" is based on a true story, again from World War II. Then there's "Laughter." Have you listened to people laugh?

CORNUCOPIA

The corner store is the crossroads of the world.
The checkout counter, bar code scanner, sacks
And impulse items — even sale sheets curled
Around the green tiled post behind the racks
Of magazines — all are entree to the soul
Which reigns within. Coffee from Brazil,
Tea from China, Indian rice, and a whole
Assortment of Italian pastas that fill
Extensive shelves to join Arabian dates,
Asian spices, Cuban sugar, Danish
Cookies, Hawaiian pineapple, and crates
Of melons from the Philippines: to wish
For something is to get it!

SIMPLICITY

The joys of life reside in simple things:
In cooling breezes, sun, in air
That hints of rain, in apples, cherries, pears
Picked ripe, and mountain streams, and crooked pines.
I revel in a sunset, mists that crown
A peak, in endless fields of waving grain,
In wooded hills, and rivers flowing free.
I cherish smiles and kindly words, a hand-
Clasp and warm comradeship, the strength of age,
The glow of youth, and childhood's saucy ways.

THE OLDS

Have you heard the olds?
The dawn broke clear at six
And globes of dew glistened
On my slippered feet.
The coffee in my mug
Was fragrant, rich, and warm,
Prelude to the toast
That awaited me inside.
Then off to class, to teach
Till four, then on to house
And hearth and kids and wife.
Sometimes we met with friends
To talk and plan and work
Till bedtime lured us home.
Then heaven on earth to fold
Her in my arms to love,
To sleep, to dream, to face
Another day, the same,
Yet always fresh, unspoiled.
My father knew the game.
I often heard him say,
"Drink up! The well is deep."
The olds is always there,
You see, the stuff of life
That needs not much of news.

SELF-SACRIFICE

Some say to me that self is sin,
That moral duty must begin
With simple self-denial in
The service of one's kith and kin.
Such thinking is quite clearly thin,
For I observe beneath the skin
Of everyone, a self, my twin:
The service of the self is sin,
It seems, only if the self's within.

("Love of one's neighbor is not possible without
love of oneself."

Herman Hesse)

OR I DIE

The violet at the window gropes for light,
Its purple head peeps out from indoor night.
If, when watering, in apparent spite
I turn the pot half round, within the sight
Of one sun's pass, or two, the plant will fight
To face its source of warmth, of life and might.
The violet at the window must have light.

LIFE'S LOTTERY

The wheel of fortune spins both good and bad
To all alike. There are no favorites,
Saint and sinner live through jars and joys
Each day and hour. From Job to Wallenberg
The story is the same. Good men — God's men
And women — often lose their bets when black
Comes up instead of red, and hail or drouth
Destroys a summer's work . . . or cancer strikes . . .
Or unemployment . . . death of spouse or child . . .
When drunken drivers slaughter innocents,
Or drug-crazed minors terrorize a town.
It might as well have been rich grain-filled bins,
Trim sun-tanned bodies, thriving crowded hearths,
Clean peaceful streets and happy schools.
It might as well have been a world at peace
Where truth and goodness really do prevail,
And justice reigns for poor as well as rich.
The lots of life fall where they will. And men
And women win or lose the game each day.
Does wisdom come through suffering? Is God
The god of good and not of ill? Does faith
Prepare men's hearts and minds to take the shocks
In stride when joys dissolve in want and tears?
Will "sovereignty" suffice? Can I with Job
Declare "Thy will is mine," and fret no more
For loss and pain quite undeserved? Can I
In patience suffer prison, punishment
And death while God seems silent and aloof?
I do not know. I only know that love
Is best, and love in action is the way
To peace on earth, for strength to meet the quirks
Of chance that force themselves on us each day.

ANGEL UNAWARE

There was a knock on the door, Tim,
A gentle cautious knock. I froze.
I was in a basement, alone,
The remnant of a house within
The battle zone in Europe. My toes
And fingers were like ice. The stone

Walls glistened with rime frost.
It was Christmas Eve, and I
Was duty radioman that night.
I had no fuel and often lost
Myself in thoughts of home. I'd try
To think of scenes of warmth and light.

I had not eaten for three days
And enemy lines were near at hand.
I heard the guns and knew I could
Be overrun at any time. The ways
Of war are strange. But I would stand
In place. Despite my fear, I would.

It came again. A stronger knock.
Who could that be? Could it be
An enemy patrol? Were lines of men
Approaching silently to block
Our soldiers in their key
Positions at the front? Again

The sound. I wondered what to do.
Answer? Ignore the sound? I stood
In silence yet awhile, then drifted
Slowly, rifle ready, to
The door. I opened it a good
Half inch to peek, before I lifted

Up the chain inside the door.
I stared amazed at what I saw.
A little girl, golden haired
With sparkling eyes of blue, no more
Than eight years old, stood there. In awe
I opened wide the door. She shared

The landing with a man, her father,
And pulled a little wagon filled
With coal. She carried in her hand
A loaf of bread. I waited, rather
Breathless at the scene, until
She said, "My name iss Hilda, and

Ve bring you gifts on Christmas Eve."
I was stunned. This dear man
And girl had risked their lives to bring
Me food and warmth. They might receive
Their death if they ignored the ban
Enforced on fraternizing.

Whenever Christmas comes, between
Times too, I think of Hilda's voice,
"My name iss Hilda," and see her face,
Enshrined in memory. The queen
 Of heav'n shines not more fair. What choice
Mem'ries then flood my soul apace.

(A friend told this story)

83

LAUGHTER

Laughter sprung from joy
Is like
Pure gold without alloy.

Laughter wrung from pain
Is like
A rainbow during rain.

Laughter with a friend
Is like
A treasure without end.

Laughter without mirth
Is like
Conception without birth.

Laughter insincere
Is like
A sob without a tear.

SKIN DEEP

Incredible skin
Keeps the insides in.
No water leaks
From melon cheeks.
No juices flow
When apples glow.

An orange, mind,
Securely binds
The sea confined
Within its rind.

That fragile skin
So paper-thin
Yet iron in
Its regimen
And discipline
Keeps all within.

WATCHING FACES

Walk the streets and search the faces,
Sense the burdens, catch the graces
Flashed in fleeting smiles, grimaces,
From each passerby.

Placid surfaces on faces
Oft belie the desperate races
Run behind the dark fringed laces
On a pair of eyes.

Behind some still and passive faces
Cauldrons seethe in secret places —
Not the kinds of commonplaces
You'd expect to find

Frozen smiles on frozen faces
Numb the terror at the bases
Of distracted minds, faint traces
Of the hidden scene.

Walk the streets and watch those faces,
Proper masks, like ancient vases
Silent sounds from inner spaces —
Enigmatic planes.

GREAT AND SMALL

The dandelion and the rose
Attest an artist's ways;
The lion's teeth and curling bud
Delight our steady gaze.

The dandelion sprinkles lawns
Insistently with gold,
Affirming immortality,
Surviving from of old.

The dandelion fills its place
With modest dignity;
Its head held high, it greets the eye
With perfect symmetry.

The rose seems fragile, seems so weak,
Yet often lives with frost;
It bravely peeps from sheltering leaves
When other blooms are lost.

The rose is monarch of all blooms,
Its fragrance fills the air,
Its regal blossom rules the field
In grace beyond compare.

The dandelion and the rose
Attest an artist's ways;
The lion's teeth and curling bud
Declare their maker's praise.

COLOPHON

At Home in Kansas is largely a reprint of my first three books of poetry, all of them out of print. *Not By Bread Alone* (1982) was followed by *Reflections on Life: Birth to Death* (1987) and that by *Tracings* (1989), all of them issued in small numbers that quickly sold out. I have herein selected those poems that seemed worthy of sharing more widely.

This present volume joins two others that deal with Kansas: . . . *and the Kansas Wind Blows* (1991) and *Prairie Sketches* (1992). In 1994 I published *Thy Love Is Better Than Wine*, a collection of sonnets on life and love.

As *At Home In Kansas* joins the series; may it bring enjoyment to each reader. For pleasure is the surest reward of poetry.

My son, Stan Nelson, is a Museum Specialist at the National Museum of American History (Smithsonian) in Washington, D.C. His lovely linoleum block illustrations grace these pages much as his line drawings and scratchboard art informed three earlier books in this father-son series.

The type face is Janson, printed on 60# Springhill Offset Smooth cream paper